LAUGH OUT LOUD!

THE OUTER SPACE JOKE BOOK

Sean Connolly and Kay Barnham

WINDMILL BOOKS

New York

Published in 2012 by Windmill Books, LLC
303 Park Avenue South, Suite # 1280, New York, NY 10010-3657

First Edition

Editor: Joe Harris
Illustrations: Adam Clay
Layout Design: Notion Design

Library of Congress Cataloging-in-Publication Data

Connolly, Sean, 1956–
 The outer space joke book / by Sean Connolly and Kay Barnham. — 1st ed.
     p. cm. — (Laugh out loud!)
Includes index.
ISBN 978-1-61533-364-6 (library binding) — ISBN 978-1-61533-402-5 (pbk.) — ISBN 978-1-61533-465-0
(6-pack)
1. Outer space—Juvenile humor. I. Barnham, Kay. II. Title.
PN6231.S645C65 2012
818'.602—dc22
                              2010052140
Printed in China

For more great fiction and nonfiction, go to www.windmillbooks.com

CPSIA Compliance Information: Batch #AS2011WM: For Further Information contact Windmill Books, New York, New York at 1-866-478-0556
SL001838US

CONTENTS

OUTER SPACE

Where do you find black holes?
In black socks.

What makes you think my son could be an astronaut?
He has nothing but space between his ears!

Did you hear about the woman who went in for plastic surgery, and came out looking like a Martian?
She told the surgeon she wanted to look like a million dollars, so he made her face all green and crinkly!

Which weighs the most, a full Moon or a half Moon?
A half Moon, because a full Moon is much lighter!

How do you get a baby astronaut
to go to sleep?
Rocket.

OUTER SPACE

Knock knock.
Who's there?
Jupiter.
Jupiter who?
Jupiter spaceship
on my lawn?

Teacher: William,
how fast does light
travel?
William: I don't
know—it's already
arrived by the time I
wake up!

Which is the most glamorous planet?
Saturn. It has a lot of rings.

When can you be sure that the Moon won't eat you?
When it's a full Moon.

What crazy bug lives on the Moon?
The lunar tick.

An astronaut and a chimp were fired off into space. The chimp opened its sealed orders, read them, and immediately started programming the flight computer. The astronaut opened his sealed orders and found only one instruction:

"Feed the chimp!"

How do aliens go fishing?
With Earthworms!

What's the center of gravity?
The letter V.

Why do little green men have nice, warm homes?
Because they live in little greenhouses!

OUTER SPACE

Why didn't the astronaut get burned when he landed on the Sun?
He went there at night!

Why are parties on the Moon always so dull?
There's no atmosphere.

Why do astronomers always bang their heads?
It helps them to see stars!

Book spotted in the school library:
Is There Life on Mars? by Howard I. No

Three badly made robots were playing cards.
The first one threw his hand in.
The second one rolled his eyes.
The third one laughed his head off.

Why don't astronauts keep their jobs for long?
Because after their training they're always fired.

What did one rocket say to the other?
I wish I could quit smoking!

Some meteorites collide with planets. What do you call meteorites that miss?
Meteowrongs.

Why did the alien turn the restaurant staff upside down?
Someone told him that you had to tip the waiter!

What did one asteroid say to the other asteroid?
"Pleased to meteor."

What do aliens cook their breakfasts on?
Unidentified frying objects.

What do young astronauts sit on during takeoff?
Booster seats.

How does the Solar System hold up its pants?
With an asteroid belt.

What did the boy star say to the girl star?
Do you want to glow out with me?

Why did the alien build a spaceship from feathers?
He wanted to travel light years!

What is an alien's favorite type of snack?
A Martian-mallow.

OUTER SPACE

Why do astronauts have to prepare a meal before blastoff?
They get hungry at launch time.

Why do astronauts make good football players?
They know how to make a great touchdown!

Why was the thirsty astronaut loitering near the computer keyboard?
He was looking for the space bar.

Big alien: If this planet is Mars, what's that one over there?
Little alien: Is it Pa's?

OUTER SPACE

What did the metric alien say to the human?
"Take me to your liter."

Did you know that they have found life on another planet?
Really?
Yes, there are fleas on Pluto!

What holds the Moon up?
Moon beams.

Why is an alien such a good gardener?
Because he has two green thumbs.

Why are grandma's teeth like stars?
Because they come out at night.

Where do you leave your spaceship when you visit another planet?
At a parking meteor!

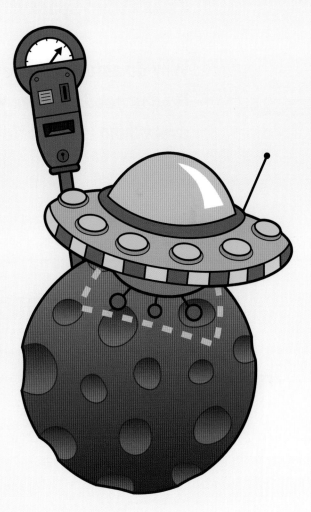

OUTER SPACE

Why do cats hate flying saucers?
Because they can't reach the milk!

What's an astronomer?
A night watchman with a college education.

Which actor won the Martian Oscars?
Kevin Outer-Spacey!

Why do astronauts never diet?
No one needs to lose weight in space, because everything is weightless!

Why did the spaceship land outside my bedroom?
You must have left the landing light on!

What's an
alien's favorite
drink?
Gravi-tea.

What did
Saturn say when
Jupiter asked if he
could call him?
"Don't call me—I'll
give you a ring."

What's normal eyesight for
a Martian?
20-20-20!

What should you do if you see a spaceman?
Park your car in it, man!

I don't know what to buy my pal, the space alien, for his
birthday.
How about five and a half pairs of slippers?

What does an alien gardener do with his hedges?
Eclipse them every spring!

Why did the alien launch a clock into space?
He wanted to see time fly.

How did the alien tie his shoelaces?
With an astro-knot.

Why don't aliens celebrate each other's birthdays?
They don't like to give away their presents.

OUTER SPACE

What's faster than the speed of light?
The speed of dark!

Who is a robot's favorite cartoon character?
Tin-tin!

When is a window like a star?
When it's a skylight.

If an athlete gets athlete's foot, what does an astronaut get?
Missile toe!

What is woolly and comes from outer space?
A ewe-F-O.

OUTER SPACE

How did the aliens hurt the farmer?
They landed on his corn.

What do you call an overweight alien?
An extra-cholesterol.

First astronomer: Do you think there's intelligent life out there?
Second astronomer: I doubt it. All the aliens I've met are pretty stupid!

Why did the robot go crazy?
He had a screw loose.

Why couldn't the alien's spaceship travel at the speed of light?
Because he took off in the dark!

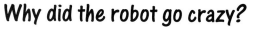

OUTER SPACE

What do you call a sick space monster?
An ailin' alien.

Spotted on the science shelf of the school library:
Fly Me to the Moon
by Tay Cough

Why did the boy become an astronaut?
Because his teacher told him he was no earthly good.

Why are astronauts such successful people?
They always go up in the world.

Which is more useful, the Sun or the Moon?
The Moon—because it shines at night when you want the light. The Sun shines during the day, when you don't really need it!

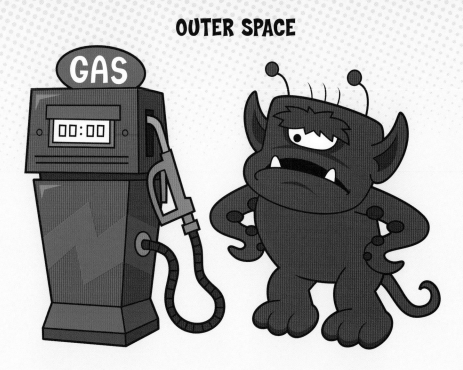

What did the alien say to the gas pump?
"Don't you know that it's rude to stick your finger in your ear when I'm talking to you?"

I've given up on time travel.
Why?
There's no future in it.

Living on Earth may be expensive—but it does include a free trip around the Sun each year.

Why are there no Martian tourists at the Grand Canyon?
Because it looks so much like home!

How do you phone the Sun?
You use a Sun-dial.

Mars got sent to prison after the big robbery trial.
Why? He wasn't even there!
Yes, but he helped to planet.

What is a light year?
The same as a normal year,
but with fewer calories.

**What did the astronaut say to his
alien girlfriend?**
"You're out of this world!"

**What do astronauts wear
in bed?**
Space jammies.

How do aliens stay clean?
They take meteor showers.

OUTER SPACE

What is an alien's favorite board game?
Moon-opoly!

How do astronauts serve drinks?
In sunglasses.

How do aliens keep from falling over in a spaceship?
They Klingon.

Why do astronauts find it hard to mix with other people?
They're not really down to Earth.

Why does Superman wear such big shoes?
Because of his amazing feats.

Clones are
people, two.

Have you seen the movie about
toads in space?
It's called Star Warts.

What is an astronaut's favorite music?
Rocket and roll.

Did you hear about the resentful robot?
He had a microchip on his shoulder.

What should you do if you meet a little green man?
Come back when he's a little riper.

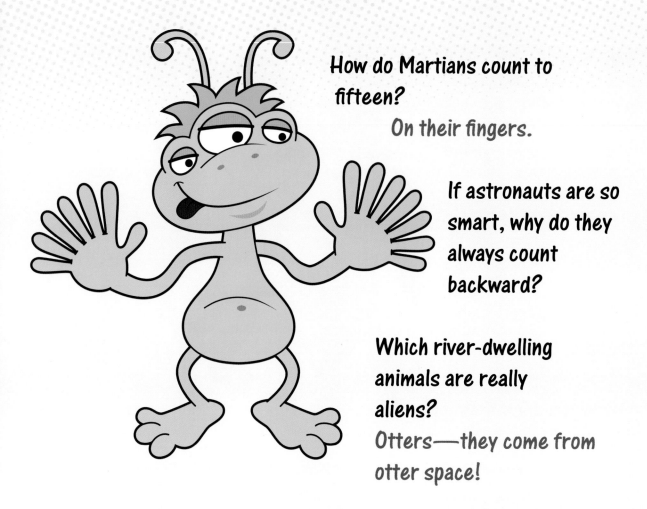

How do Martians count to fifteen?

On their fingers.

If astronauts are so smart, why do they always count backward?

Which river-dwelling animals are really aliens?

Otters—they come from otter space!

How many Martians does it take to screw in a light bulb? Millions! One to hold the bulb, and the rest to turn the planet.

What did the loser in the astronomy contest receive? The constellation prize.

OUTER SPACE

Which relative visits astronauts in outer space?
Auntie Gravity.

Sign on town hall notice board:
"The lecture on time travel will be held two weeks ago."

First ground controller: Man, that astronaut is totally crazy.
Second ground controller: Yes, he's a real space cadet!

Which are the dreamiest scientists?
Astronomers, because they have stars in their eyes.

What happened to the astronaut who stepped on chewing gum?
He got stuck in orbit.

OUTER SPACE

What's crunchy and travels at 10,000 miles an hour?
A space chip!

What do you call a laser gun with low batteries?
A flashlight.

First Martian, just landed in Texas: Which do you think is farther away, New York or the Moon?
Second Martian: Don't be silly—can you see New York from here?

How do Martians shave?
With laser blades.

What did the alien say to the cat?
Take me to your litter.

What goes MOOZ?
A spaceship backing up.

Why did the alien family have to move house?
Because they were all spaced out.

Knock knock!
Who's there?
Athena.
Athena who?
Athena shooting star last night.

What do aliens download on their iPods?
The Neptunes.

Which planet is shaped like a fish?
Nep-tuna.

What do you call a really noisy spaceship?
A space racket.

What did the traffic light say to the robot?
"Don't look—I'm changing."

What do you call an egg from outer space?
An Unidentified Flying Omelet.

What do giant aliens do with astronauts?
They put them in the store cupboard, with all the other canned food!

What lightweight tool can you use to fix a spaceship?
A pocket rocket sprocket!

How is an alien crop circle like a lame joke?
Because they're both corny.

What did the greedy alien say?
"Take me to your larder!"

What do meteors like to read?
Comet books!

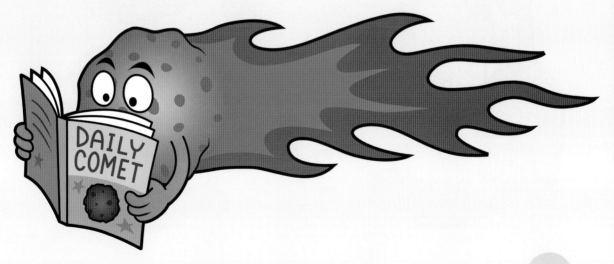

OUTER SPACE

How many planets are out in space?
All of them.

Why are astronauts big fans of Michael Jackson?
He taught them how to moonwalk.

What injections do sick rockets get?
Booster shots.

What did the Martian painter say to the Earth painter?
Take me to your ladder.

What did the romantic Moon monster say to his girlfriend?
"Let's go for a walk—there's a beautiful Earth out tonight."

How is the Moon like a dollar?
Because it has four quarters.

Why is the space program such good value?
Because people's tax dollars go farther than ever before.

What kind of extraterrestrial villain works in a restaurant?
Darth Waiter.

Why was the spaceship bent?
It had been traveling at warp speed.

How do you find a cow in space?
Follow the Milky Way.

How many ears does Captain Kirk have?
Three—a right ear, a left ear, and a final frontier!

Why did the steel robot have so many friends?
It must have been his magnetic personality!

Where do Martians go for a drink?
To a Mars bar.

Why was Pluto squashed flat?
Because Mars Saturn Pluto!

What do astronauts wear on their day off?
Apollo shirts.

How is medicine packaged for astronauts?
In space capsules.

Pupil: I want to be an astronaut when I grow up.
Teacher: Well, you certainly have high hopes!

Knock knock!
Who's there?
Detail.
Detail who?
De-tail is de-end
of de-comet.

How do you say
farewell to a
two-headed
alien?
"Bye bye
bye bye!"

Glossary

astronomer (ah-STRON-oh-mur)
a scientist who studies outer
space

atmosphere (AT-moss-feer) the
gases that surround a planet

calories (KAL-oh-reez) units that
are used to measure the energy
in food

cholesterol (kuh-LESS-tuh-roll) a
fatty substance found in foods
like cheese, eggs, and meat

extraterrestrial (EX-truh-tuh-RESS-
tree-ull) from somewhere other
than planet Earth

sprocket (SPROK-it) a machine part
that looks like a small wheel with
teeth around the rim

Further Reading

Byrne, John. *Teachers Are from Mars,
Pupils Are from Venus.* New York:
Red Fox Books, 2001.

Li, Amanda *Intergalactic! 150
Cosmic Jokes About Space.*
New York: Macmillan, 2009.

Woo, Diane. *Space and Alien
Jokes That Are Out of This World.*
New York: Tor Books, 2010.

Index

Web Sites

For Web resources related to
the subject of this book, go to:
www.windmillbooks.com/weblinks
and select this book's title.